TOMORROW'S WORLD WITH INFORMATION TECHNOLOGY

SARATH KUMAR S

Contents

Contents

Preface

The future is near. The strategic use of information and technology is continuing to transform the world. Consumers are demanding more. They want constant, uninterrupted connection to information services through the systems in their homes, their vehicles, personal digital assistants, computing networks and even appliances. Businesses are expanding in new directions to drive lean, strategic operations that link to customers, suppliers and partners-instantaneously sensing and adapting to changes in the supply chain network. Products once delivered as stand-alones now harbor embedded technologies, allowing them to meld into an integrated flow of information and services.

But as remarkable as this future looks, two questions remain: What is the role of IT in this future new world? In the new world order, true success will depend on an IT organization's ability to split its technology mindset, focusing both on technology and on a forward-looking business strategy. This new thinking begins by stabilizing mature applications and speeding the maturation process to refocus resources and efforts where they matter most on creating business value.

CHAPTER ONE

I.T - Business Perspective

Increasingly, there is a disconnect between the way IT views the organization and the way the business views IT. While more than 70 percent of business executives think their business strategies are highly dependent on information technology, few consider the source of that success to be in their IT functions.

The same research also illustrates how executives view the future. For example, executives think information assets and technology solutions are crucial to their competitive differentiation in the marketplace. And they know that innovation in products and services as well as the value chain will differentiate them in the marketplace. At the same time, they do not believe the source of technology innovation is found in their IT organizations. Indeed, 72 percent of executives say technology innovation is typically found within the business-well outside the IT organization. Further, the cost and time it takes to integrate innovative solutions with their existing IT infrastructures often causes more problems. In short, the IT organization does not deliver its full value to the enterprise.

Increasingly, business leaders are focused on the future while most IT organizations are rooted in today, contemplating new ways to cut costs and improve efficiencies. Yet rather than focusing solely on driving the last penny of waste out of their own organizations, IT organizations should be finding ways to help their companies improve business operations and create new growth opportunities.

CHAPTER TWO

Focus & Effort on "Value"

Telling someone to focus on value is a far cry from doing it. Today's IT organizations are simply not structured to focus on value. IT organizations tend to be segmented by functional areas, with applications in each function maintained by a support structure of dedicated analysts and programmers. Within this approach, organizations treat all of their IT assets alike. A mature asset gets the same level of support as an asset that increases business value despite the fact that the latter asset has the potential to create significant value for the company. For example, many companies over-invest in mature financial applications that offer limited competitive value. After all, there is a finance programming staff and a yearly budget that must be spent. These same companies will under-invest in the challenging architectural foundation necessary to support an improved customer capability or digital products.

How can the IT organization focus resources and effort on improving business value? Let's go through those steps:

1) Strategic Priorities
2) Maturation of Current Technologies
3) Manage Strategic Technologies

CHAPTER THREE

Strategic Priorities

It may sound intuitive, but the first step to improving IT's value contribution to the overall business is understanding where you are today. Are you paying attention to the strategic priorities of the business? Is your IT portfolio segmented in a way that will increase business value and competitive advantage?

Answers to these questions can be ascertained by a thorough assessment of your IT portfolio-examining each set of functional applications and segmenting them based on their strategic value, competitive capability and your current budget. Once the portfolio is segmented, you'll have a clearer view of investment priorities.

Typically, the assessment is the point at which companies find they are over-investing in mature applications and under-investing in applications that have the potential to deliver strategic value. The goal is to refocus resources on the high value, differentiating technologies. But before resources can be sent elsewhere, the company must free-up resources from the mature or maturing areas. This leads to the second step.

CHAPTER FOUR

Maturation of Current Technologies

All technologies mature over time, which means they become standardized and usually require fewer resources and smaller budgets. It is important to appropriately manage the maturing process. Top companies move quickly to trim their support of mature functions and look for ways to accelerate the process. How a company manages its mature technologies is often the key to freeing up investments for new business opportunities.

There are several ways to force the maturation of current technologies. Some companies choose outsourcing. Others turn the process over to outside service providers. Still others choose to go it alone. But regardless of approach, the key is to drive down long-term maintenance and support costs while providing an adaptable architecture that can easily accommodate new enhancements and new technologies. Even in the most mature applications, you should anticipate and expect the development of new technologies and new interfaces or extensions. For example, financial applications will likely need to accommodate new forms of electronic payments and new interfaces to partners.

CHAPTER FIVE

Manage Strategic Technologies

New technologies are on our doorstep. How many possible ways can you communicate with your customers in their cars? How will ubiquitous IP change your IT infrastructure? How will multiple technologies merge together to change your business?

Clearly, IT should be leading the way in generating valuable business solutions. Yet, as mentioned earlier, the majority of executives think their best technology ideas are generated outside of their IT organizations. This is not good news for IT organizations. How can IT executives change business executives' minds? One way is to first change the mindset of the IT organization. Rather than focusing solely on technologies, it is time to concentrate efforts on finding business solutions as well. An IT organization that has a solid understanding of the business and can offer potential solutions to business problems, will be better able to help the company capture value.

One key to success is collaboration. Indeed, an IT organization that works cooperatively with the business can lead an innovation agenda. The process should begin with creating a "roadmap" of current and future technologies based on where they are in the maturity cycle and the potential business solutions they enable. Discuss the technology roadmap-along with the portfolio segmentation-with business leaders to come up with new solutions that will enhance the value of the business. The technology roadmap will help push thinking in new directions. Working together, IT and business leaders will determine how technology can be used to generate business value.

CHAPTER SIX

Career in Information Technology

IT students have a lot of scope for their future. Since the technologies and IT sectors are increasing day by day, the need of employers are also increasing. But just reaching IT field for the sake of a degree and a job wont give success. Because in coming future the IT industries do not adopt employers having degrees for a short term course, they need really talented and well experienced employers to do their job.

According to Oxford Advanced Learner's dictionary, Information Technology is "the study or use of electronic equipment, especially computers, for storing, accessing, analysing and sending information". This means that the students choosing this field have to deal with many things like the infrastructure, development, storage, processing, and networking of devices apart from exchanging various forms of electronic data and its security. In fact, security to the future of IT.

Some of the most popular and mind-boggling ideas which are running on the wheels of IT are:

- Social media networking
- Patient portals
- Digital marketing
- Mobile Applications
- Website Applications
- Online shopping Portals
- Internet Banking

CHAPTER SEVEN

Capitalizing on the New Normal

The current Covid-19 pandemic has disrupted the world in unimaginable ways. From businesses to lifestyles and livelihoods, the outbreak has upended our lives overnight. For businesses across verticals, this has led to an unprecedented downfall in revenues and operations with extended lockdowns in several countries. Some industries such as travel and aviation, retail, and hospitality have taken the worst hit due to lockdowns, travel restrictions, and a significant slump in consumer spending. However, even amidst this economic crisis, some of the niche sectors have not only managed to stay afloat but also witness trend-defying growth. Capitalising on the new normal, these sectors have recorded an increase in their revenues and customer base. Let us, then, look at the top 5 niche sectors that are enjoying a booming business despite the economic fall.

CHAPTER EIGHT

Ed-Tech

Since the onset of the pandemic and the subsequent lockdowns, the ed-tech industry has seen a considerable upsurge in users. With schools and colleges shut, ed-tech has been the savior for teachers, students, and parents as well. Innovative and interactive teaching methods such as live classes, on-the-spot doubt clearance, and practice papers are offering a fulfilling learning experience for students. Not just students, the demand for skill-based and knowledge-based online courses has also soared among salaried professionals. This rise in demand for both students and professionals is undoubtedly accelerating the growth of ed-tech.

CHAPTER NINE

Online Gaming

With people being forced to remain indoors and maintain social distancing from others, they need to keep themselves occupied. Online gaming has come to their rescue. The pandemic has offered a boost to the gaming industry. With innumerable options to choose from and several new trends such as the rise of AR and VR, gaming is now all about the experience, and players in the industry are determined to offer a highly immersive and captivating experience.

CHAPTER TEN

Agri-Tech

Home to over 1.3 billion people, over 50% of India's population is involved in the agricultural sector. One of the reasons agriculture is still taking precedence even during the global crisis is that food can never go out of business it's a fundamental aspect of our survival! However, agriculture cannot power through the pandemic and the future on its own and needs cutting-edge technology. The Covid-19 crisis has paved the way for large-scale digitization in this sector and agri-tech has steadily been gaining traction, as a result. With traditional marketing channels disrupted, farmers are now accessing digital mandis to directly connect with wholesale buyers and sell their produce from the safety and comfort of their homes. Even online grocers have turned to the digital mandis to get seamless access to fresh produce. Considering that the availability of food, or the lack thereof, will definitely impact mankind, agri-tech is one of the industries which will thrive.

CHAPTER ELEVEN

Med-Tech

As we see healthcare systems across the globe stretched worryingly thin, the role of med-tech in cushioning the impact cannot be stressed enough. From infra-red thermometers to lifesaving ventilators, med-tech has aided the medicine industry at every step. Other than that, the influx of cloud-based storage solutions has helped doctors, researchers and healthcare institutes to manage the overwhelming amount of paperwork and documentation in recent times. Telemedicine is another area of med-tech that has emerged as a savior of patients, enabling them to consult with doctors virtually. This has been particularly helpful for people from remote areas and tier-II and tier-III cities. Taking into account the mayhem induced by the pandemic, it is no surprise that the med-tech industry has observed a surge in business.

CHAPTER TWELVE

Online Media

Spending over 90% of their time indoors, people are constantly looking for quality content to consume. In today's digital world, online content is the king. The pandemic has paved the way for the online media and entertainment industry to achieve inexplicable growth. OTT platforms such as Netflix, Amazon Prime, and Hotstar are seeing a significant rise in the percentage of viewers. With movie theatres and other avenues of entertainment such as concerts being temporarily banned, even stars from the entertainment industry have taken to online platforms. Without a shadow of a doubt, these industries are the ones who are making the most out of the pandemic with almost the entire world's population turning to them. Their heightened demand signifies that they are prospering and the road ahead for these sectors is promising. Their heightened demand signifies that they are prospering and the road ahead for these sectors is promising. So from this we came to know that IT has never stopped even in the covid situation. We have been hearing in news every day that there has been a pandemic impact on IT industries. So there is constant growth going on in any market, there is no fun in it, there should be a stop above so that gives us courage. If someone falls as low as he can but has clear goals and vision, he will go higher and get success. So Similar Situations of IT Industries also, we all know that the future is going to be in IT from every side.

CHAPTER THIRTEEN

Necessary in Business

Over the years, technology has caused an explosion in commerce and trade. Because of technology, many traditional business models and concepts were revolutionized. Technology gave us the opportunity to see things from a new perspective, and to approach what we were already doing from a new perspective. Technology also gave us greater efficiency for conducting business.

Some of the areas in which technology is crucial to business include point of sales systems, the use of ICT in management, accounting systems, and other complex aspects of every day business activities. Even something as simple as the calculator, which was revolutionary in its time, came about because of technology. It is tough to imagine going back to performing tasks manually. It would take us back about 100 or so years.

CHAPTER FOURTEEN

Source of Support & Security

Technology enables us to automate numerous processes, which thereby increases our productivity. This is possible because it enables us to use fewer resources, thereby enabling us to improve on quality at a low cost and to improve the speed with which we can deliver to customers. In the process, it has become possible to serve even more clients.

Technology also makes it easy to store more information while maintaining the integrity of that information. We are better able to store sensitive and confidential information in a way that makes it less vulnerable to a data breach. The information can be retrieved instantly when needed, and it can be analyzed not only to study past trends but also to forecast the future. In turn, this can help with the decision-making process.

CHAPTER FIFTEEN

Link to the World

Communication is a part of business. So, transportation and processes make business a web of complicated processes that interplay with each other. With technology, it has been possible to globalize business operations. Now, just about anyone can do business practically anywhere, from any room in their house..

Technology has made it possible for businesses to have a wider reach in the world. The best example of this is the internet and the World Wide Web. The internet is now a crucial part of any businesses' marketing campaign, as it enables the business to attract customers world wide.

Technology, when well-integrated with business, has made life itself worth living. It would be foolish to deny, however, that there are also threats to business brought about by technology. These include malicious activities by activities and organizations, such as hacking. Because of this, it is important for businesses to exercise responsibility when using technology to conduct business. With the good that technology brings, there is some bad that must also be dealt with. All the same, it is something that's worth all of the baggage, and we must acknowledge and responsibly utilize it to make our businesses better.

CHAPTER SIXTEEN

The Advent of Mobile Solutions

Mobility is seen by many as the next great frontier for businesses. Google's algorithms reflect this, as they make mobile websites a priority. Your business, and every aspect of it can be handled, using nothing more than a tablet or smartphone. From content marketing to customer relations, to sales, the back-end stuff like invoicing and shipping , all of that power is in your hands.

But mobile solutions aren't just about businesses; they are also about consumers. The millennial generation uses their phones to do everything from buying and selling to sharing their experiences with their friends and finding local businesses.

CHAPTER SEVENTEEN

The Phenomenon of Cloud Computing

Cloud computing has made it possible for businesses to outsource many of their functions to third parties using the internet. It makes it possible for variable data packages to be handled but also makes it possible for businesses to expand rapidly and embrace mobility without having to worry about such things as crashes, downtime, and lost data. This has enabled small and medium-sized businesses to gain access to resources that would have cost them a fortune only a few years ago. In effect, the playing field has been leveled.

CHAPTER EIGHTEEN

Increased Customer Segmentation

Since more and more data is flowing, it is now much easier to analyze and gain deep insight into the things that customers are looking for. Analytics services are expanding by the day and are allowing businesses to segment their prospects into more and more specific groups, making it much easier to target them and get more value for their advertising money. Something as simple as having a Google account can let a business know where a user is from, the kind of browser they're using, how they stumbled upon a website, What they do on that website, how long they are likely to stay and at what point they decide to leave. There are even more advanced analytics services that allow businesses to become even more refined with this segmentation in order to improve their conversions drastically.

CHAPTER NINETEEN

Increased Connectivity

Technology has made it easier for people to stay in touch. Whether you're looking to communicate with your employees and colleagues via video chat or sending email blasts to leads, mobile technology and the constant innovation that takes place within the space has made it possible for communication to take on a new level of hyper-realism.

CHAPTER TWENTY

Decreasing Costs and Increasing Utility

There are two main things that have come together to make what is called a "buyer's market" possible. These are the fact that both hardware and software that are needed in creating the necessary software solutions have become more affordable and the fact that more and more entrepreneurs who are also tech-savvy are appearing by the day to make use of these technologies. There was a time when it would take a large company about a year to build a back-end inventory system. Now it takes a few college graduates a matter of weeks to build the same thing. Since the solutions are offered affordably and very easy to use, businesses do not have to invest too much money into them and that has made business easier.

CHAPTER TWENTY-ONE

A Changing Consumer Base

Millennials have come of age and they are now the force driving the modern economy. Pretty soon, over half the American workforce will consist of millennials and pretty soon they will also be coming into their peak affluence, where they will have a lot of money to spend and very few financial obligations, give them a lot of disposable income. They are greater in number than the baby boomers and are a lot more liberal with their wallets. They are also all about instant gratification. They have also been raised with the internet. They are connected, tech-savvy, and ready to spend. Businesses have to adapt to this new customer base if they are going to thrive.

CHAPTER TWENTY-TWO

Greater Consideration for the Social Impact of Business

You can't just assume your business operates in a vacuum anymore. Social networking has made the world a smaller place where users can connect regardless of who they are, where they're from, and how wealthy they are. Only a few years ago you could have gotten by if your customer service was just okay. Now you have to put in the extra effort if you don't want unfavorable ratings on review sites and people going on rants on social media about your service. Businesses, therefore, need to be careful about their online reputation and need to work on their digital footprint.

CHAPTER TWENTY-THREE

The End of Downtime

This is actually a negative effect of technology. With increased connectivity, individuals have less and less time to themselves now. Vacation seems to have all but become a thing of the past, with most people working even when they're on vacation. Since we can always access our emails, texts, and social media through our phones and laptops, it is harder and harder to just disconnect and wind down.

CHAPTER TWENTY-FOUR

Why Is I.T Important to an Organization?

It might be a little difficult to fathom the importance of information technology to an organization if you're not an IT professional. However, there are numerous ways in which information technology is crucial to an organization.

Business

The business world changed forever when computers were introduced onto the scene. Businesses can utilize information technology through the use of computers and different software to run their operations in a smoother fashion. They use it in different departments, including finance, manufacturing, human resources, and security.

Education

Education is one of the frontiers of technology and is growing with technology every day. It's important that education be able to keep up with the progress happening in technology by reaching students in a way that adequately helps them to prepare for the future. The students in our classrooms today are meant to be the thought leaders, business people, teachers, and investors of tomorrow, so technology should be used to prepare them. This includes the use of gadgets in teaching, such as computers, mobile phones, and tablets, as well as the use of the internet as a medium of learning.

Finance

With an increasing number of transactions happening online, it is important that financial and security institutions work together to make the internet a safe place. As more transactions are done on the internet, there will be a need for more networks and greater security, making it possible for banks to keep purchases and sales secure.

Health

With improvements in information technology, it is becoming easier to reform the health sector. Medical offices are now able to share medical information with each other, and they can get your health data from your previous doctors. This makes it possible for timely care to be delivered, as well as for costs to be reduced.

Security

With an increasing number of transactions being done online, there is an ever-increasing need for safety. Information technology is what makes it possible to keep your data and information safe and only accessible by you. Through the use of encryption and passwords, your digital data is safely hidden away and can only be accessed by those who have your permission.

CHAPTER TWENTY-FIVE

Benefits to Communication

Rapid communications can help increase productivity, allow for better business decision-making and ease a company's expansion into new territories or countries. Email servers, routers, internal company billboards and chat services can serve as the backbone of a company's communications. These electronically based communication systems are used to disseminate routine and critical business information in a quick and efficient manner. IT equipment can be used to send business status reports to executives, to update employees on critical business projects and to connect with business partners and customers.

CHAPTER TWENTY-SIX

Improved Workplace Efficiency

Streamlined work flow systems, shared storage and collaborative work spaces can increase efficiency in a business and allow employees to process a greater level of work in a shorter period of time. Information technology systems can be used to automate routine tasks, to make data analysis easier and to store data in a manner that can easily be retrieved for future use. Technology can also be used to answer customer questions through email, in a real-time chat session or through a telephone routing system that connects a customer to an available customer service agent.

CHAPTER TWENTY-SEVEN

Competitive Advantage over Rivals

Adoption of information technology resources allows companies to maintain a competitive advantage over their rivals. Companies using a first-movers strategy can use information technology to create new products, distance their products from the existing market or enhance their customer services. Companies that follow a low-cost product strategy can look to information technology solutions to reduce their costs through increased productivity and reduced need for employee overhead. Businesses can also build-in information technology to their products that makes it difficult for customers to switch platforms or products.

CHAPTER TWENTY-EIGHT

Cost Reduction and Economic Efficiencies

Companies can harness information technology resources to lower their costs. Using IT infrastructure, redundant tasks can be centralized at one location. For example, a large company could centralize their payroll function at one location to lower employee costs.

Economic efficiencies can also be realized by migrating high-cost functions into an online environment. Companies can offer email support for customers that may have a lower cost than a live customer support call. Cost savings could also be found through outsourcing opportunities, remote work options and lower-cost communication options.

CHAPTER TWENTY-NINE

Broaden Customer Bases

Technology allows small businesses to reach new economic markets. Rather than just selling consumer goods or services in the local market, small businesses can reach regional, national and international markets. Retail websites are the most common way small businesses sell products in several different economic markets.

Websites represent a low-cost option that consumers can access 24/7 when needing to purchase goods or services. Small business owners can also use internet advertising to reach new markets and customers through carefully placed web banners or ads.

CHAPTER THIRTY

Collaboration and Outsourcing

Business technology allows companies to outsource business functions to other businesses in the national and international business environment. Outsourcing can help companies lower costs and focus on completing the business function they do best. Technical support and customer service are two common function companies outsource.

Small business owners may consider outsourcing some operations if they do not have the proper facilities or available manpower. Outsourcing technology also allows businesses to outsource function to the least expensive areas possible, including foreign countries.

CHAPTER THIRTY-ONE

Summary

Information technology refers to the study and development of a support-management based, computerized information system. The development is mainly observed in the form of dedicated software applications and a number of hardware programs. The advantages of IT include work place cost-effectiveness and essential globalization.

The common work environment today is totally dependent on computers. This has led to the need to develop and consistently upgrade dedicated computer software like project management software, for a number of related requirements. These include storage and protection of content, processing and transmitting of dedicated information and the secured retrieval of information, when and as required. IT promotes computing technology, covering everything from installing applications to developing databases.

All our work related applications are now completely automated, thanks to the IT sector. IT professionals are people involved in essential management of sensitive data, exclusive computer networking and systems-engineering. Things that were once done manually or by hand have now become easier and faster due to the advent of a computing technology. Our world today has changed a great deal with the aid of IT which has penetrated almost every aspect of our daily lives and society, from leisure to business. IT has become a part of our day-to-day lives through the evident use of PC's, Internet, cell phones, faxes, the list would seem endless. Let us hope that newer development in the field of IT can provide benefits to our future generations, just as it has greatly benefited ours.

Printed by Libri Plureos GmbH in Hamburg,
Germany